I0586549

Gla
Libra
nam

C0062 02761

BIG-TIME BUSINESS

ENERGY FOR EVERYONE?
THE BUSINESS OF ENERGY

Nick Hunter

FRANKLIN WATTS
LONDON • SYDNEY

First published 2015 by Franklin Watts
338 Euston Road
London NW1 3BH

Franklin Watts Australia
Level 17/207 Kent Street
Sydney, NSW 2000

© Franklin Watts 2015

All rights reserved

Produced by Calcium

A CIP catalogue record for this book is available from
the British Library.

ISBN 978 1 4451 3915 9

Dewey classification: 333.7'9

Printed in China

Franklin Watts is a division of Hachette Children's Books,
an Hachette UK company
www.hachette.co.uk

GLASGOW LIFE GLASGOW LIBRARIES	
C006202761	
StAnd	PETERS
21-Jan-2015	£12.99
T333.79	

Acknowledgements:
The publisher would like to thank the following for permission to reproduce
photographs: Cover: Shutterstock: Kayros Studio l, N.Minton cr, Mirounga cl, Valdis
Torms tcr. Inside: Dreamstime: Robert Young 15t; Library of Congress: 8br, 9br, 10c;
Shutterstock: Asharkyu 13tr, Sergei Bachlakov 33b, Baloon111 30, Darren Brode
43t, Chonlapoom 26b, Songquan Deng 12b, Tad Denson 3br, 20tr, Patrik Dietrich
19tr, Dikiiy 11b, Elnur 14–15b, esbobeldijk 42bl, Chris H. Galbraith 32tr, Richard
Griffin 11tr, Steve Heap 44cr, Left Eyed Photography 24r, Monkey Business Images
35br, 41, Jaddingt 31cl, Jordache 27l, Oleksandr Kalinichenko 18–19b, Kayros Studio
1tl, Christopher Kolaczan 37t, John Kroetch 39l, Oleksiy Mark 40bl, Ilja Mašík 5tr,
Sue McDonald 41r, Caitlin Mirra 44l, Christopher Parypa 4b, WDG Photo 28l, Rtem
17t, Veronika Rumko 5tr, Brad Sauter 16r, Jeff Schultes 6bl, Dalibor Sevaljevic 22b,
Silverkblack 23t, Vasily Smirnov 34–35tc, Michel Stevelmans 7l, Tish1 25c, Liviu Toader
13bl, Jeff Wilber 38cr, Ahmad Faizal Yahya 36b, Eldad Yitzhak 29b; US Coastguard:
Petty Officer First Class John Masson 21bl.

Every attempt has been made to clear copyright. Should there be any inadvertent
omission please apply to the publisher for rectification.

CONTENTS

POWER FOR THE PEOPLE

Energy is essential for all life. We eat food to give us the energy we need to run, jump, work and play. The products and machines that we use every day also need energy to make them work. Cars, planes and most other vehicles get their energy from burning fuel in their engines. Lights and other electrical appliances run on electricity, which is generated in power plants and brought to your home by power cables.

Big business

Energy is one of the world's biggest and most important industries. The energy business encompasses everything from finding energy sources, such as coal and oil, to supplying the energy needed to run your television or computer. This book looks at what the industry does, how it makes money and what challenges it faces in the future.

Huge amounts of coal must be burnt to create the electricity used in our cities.

IN THE NEWS

The energy industry is often in the news. Environmental campaigners accuse the business of damaging the environment. People also complain when electricity and fuel prices rise too high. However, they can do little to change the energy industry because their cars and homes depend on the energy it provides.

CHAPTER 1

THE RISE OF THE ENERGY INDUSTRY

People have always needed energy to keep them warm. Hundreds of years ago, this energy usually came from burning wood on an open fire. Ships at sea were powered by wind energy and vehicles got the energy they needed to move from the horses that pulled them. We still use horsepower as a measure of how much energy an engine can produce.

Before the invention of the engine, vehicles were powered by animals such as horses or cattle.

Today, huge amounts of energy in the form of petrol and diesel are consumed by our engine-powered cars.

The Industrial Revolution

Energy became big business during a period known as the Industrial Revolution. This began in about 1750 in Great Britain and soon spread to other countries in Europe and North America.

Production speeds up

During the Industrial Revolution new machines were invented that made it possible for factories to produce large quantities of goods, such as clothing and all sorts of metal products, very quickly. These new machines ran on steam power. Coal was used to heat up water to make the steam.

FUTURE FACT

The amount of energy that the world uses today has increased dramatically since the early days of steam power. There are more than 1 billion vehicles on the roads, and this number continues to rise as India and China become richer.

BIRTH OF THE ENERGY INDUSTRY

In the early 1800s, steam power began to be used in transport. Before long, railways were built to link cities and later they crossed whole continents. Steamships began to carry passengers across the oceans. By 1900, more than nine-tenths of the energy used by industry came from coal, and coal mining companies became some of the world's biggest businesses.

To satisfy the demand for coal, even children were recruited to work in the mines.

Electricity and gas

Fuel made from coal provided street lighting in the growing cities of the Industrial Revolution. Coal was also essential for producing electricity. The first coal-fired power stations were opened by Thomas Edison in London and New York in the early 1880s.

Striking oil

The coal industry soon had a rival. In 1859, Edwin Drake drilled the United States' first commercial oil well at Oil Creek, Pennsylvania. At first oil was used mainly to fuel oil lamps. Then came an invention in the 1890s that was to revolutionise the oil industry: the car was born.

This image from 1896 shows Oil City, founded at the mouth of Oil Creek.

SMOG

The growing energy industry rapidly changed the world. Fumes from coal burnt by industry caused smog, a thick haze of fog combined with smoke, which blackened buildings and choked the air. Many people suffered health problems as a result. We are now also discovering that burning fossil fuels, such as coal, has a long-term impact on climate (see pages 19 and 37).

TRANSPORT
AND TYCOONS

With the birth of the car in the 1890s came the need for a new energy source. Coal was fine for the large steam engines used to power trains and ships, but it was not suitable for cars, with their smaller engines. Petrol, which is made from oil, proved the ideal fuel for the car's internal combustion engine.

FUTURE FACT

Nuclear power generates about 13 per cent of the world's electricity. If this amount is to increase in the future, the energy industry will have to find solutions to nuclear power's high costs and safety issues.

Henry Ford became one of the first tycoons of the twentieth century. He was the first car manufacturer to produce cars in large quantities. This made it possible for him to sell them more cheaply than other early car manufacturers.

Money in oil

Early cars were expensive and unreliable. By 1900, there were little more than 25,000 cars worldwide. Sales took off when, in 1908, Henry Ford launched the Model T. This was a mass-produced car that ordinary people could afford to buy. As sales of cars soared and engines using oil-based fuels became standard in ships and aircraft, the corporations and business leaders that controlled the supply of oil grew very rich. Probably the most famous of these oil tycoons was John D. Rockefeller of the Standard Oil Company.

This is an early Ford car, Ford Model T 1924, on display at an exhibition of technical antiques.

THE MODERN WORLD

Coal and oil are the most important sources of energy today. Companies and countries that control supplies of oil and coal can make big profits by selling their resources to people who need energy.

The rise of gas

Gas and oil are both fossil fuels, and are often found together. In the past, the gas was burnt off and only the oil was extracted, because the gas was thought less useful than the oil and too difficult to transport. Today, however, gas is transported via pipelines and makes up about a quarter of the world's energy supply.

In areas that receive a lot of sunshine, solar power is a useful alternative energy source.

Desert cities, such as Las Vegas in the United States, use large amounts of energy just to keep buildings and cars cool enough for people to live there.

GAS WARS

Gas pipelines from Russia cross Ukraine to supply gas to Western Europe. In 2009, a dispute between Russia and Ukraine led to Russia switching off the supply of gas for two weeks. This cut the supply to Europe during freezing weather, and showed how important it is for the energy industry to remain stable.

Alternative energy sources

In 2014, the world's population reached 7.2 billion people, and it continues to rise. As it rises, the demand for energy also increases. The energy industry needs to exploit all available forms of energy, not just fossil fuels, to meet the growing demand. This has led to an increased focus on alternative sources of energy, such as solar and wind power.

CHAPTER 2

ENERGY EXPLORATION

Raw materials are the backbone of the energy industry. To meet the world's growing energy needs, the energy industry has to find the raw materials needed to generate energy. Those raw materials may be used to power cars, ships and aircraft, or to generate electricity for your home.

High risks, high costs

Searching for fossil fuels and extracting them from deep beneath Earth's surface involves huge costs. Many fossil fuels are found in places with extreme climates, and deep under the ocean bed. The people who extract the fuel must work in very difficult and dangerous conditions, such as on oil platforms far out at sea.

All the oil in some areas has been extracted. These oil wells around Baku, Azerbaijan, are now deserted.

The search for oil is now taking place in some of the most extreme parts of the planet, such as the Arctic.

New technology

As well as funding fossil fuel exploration and extraction, the energy industry must also pay for the technology needed to use other forms of energy, such as nuclear and solar energy.

FUTURE FACT

Fossil fuels are non-renewable energy sources – once they have been extracted, they are gone for good. People are worried that the oil industry has discovered enough oil to last only for the next few decades.

15

KING COAL

For many industries, coal
is the most important
source of energy. Much
of the electricity that we use
in our homes is generated
by coal-fired power stations.
Coal is also used to produce
coke, a refined form of coal.
Coke is burnt to provide
the heat needed to extract
molten iron from iron ore.
Coal is also used to make
cement, which is important
in the construction of roads,
bridges and buildings.

**Thousands of
tonnes of coal are
transported by trains
across countries.**

Today, underground coal mining relies on machinery rather than man-power.

DANGER!

In the past men, women and children mined for coal in dangerous conditions. Today most mining is done by huge cutting machines, which is safer and more efficient than methods used in the past. Disasters do still happen, though. In 2014, more than 200 miners in Turkey were involved in a mining disaster.

Surface mines

Every year, the energy industry mines about 7.7 billion tonnes of coal. Most of it comes from China, the United States, India and Australia. China is the greatest coal producer, mining around 3,826 tonnes of coal each year. Although we think of coal as coming from deep underground, it is also extracted from huge surface mines, where it lies close to ground level. Surface mining is less expensive than other mining, and more coal can be mined by each worker.

THE SEARCH FOR OIL AND GAS

Oil is not just an essential fuel for transport.
It is also important in the petrochemical industry, which produces plastics, cleaning products and many other materials from oil. Oil companies employ geologists to look for underground rock formations that may contain oil. An oil well is then drilled to reach the oil and bring it to the surface.

Oil tankers are used to transport thousands of litres of oil across the oceans.

NO SMOKING

BE ALERT AVOID POLLUTION   WORK SAFELY PREVENT ACCIDENT

SAFETY FIRST

DANGEROUS CARGO

The oil business

Much of the world's oil and gas is found beneath the deserts of countries in the Middle East. Saudi Arabia, Iran and the United Arab Emirates have all grown wealthy by exporting their oil. Elsewhere in the world, giant multinational corporations, such as ExxonMobil, Shell and BP, search and drill for oil in many different locations.

Some territories in the United Arab Emirates have huge reserves of oil.

FUTURE FACT

By burning fossil fuels, we are changing the climate. The gases that coal and oil give off when burnt change the make-up of Earth's atmosphere. To try to stop climate change, governments are backing the search for alternative fuels.

DEEP-SEA OIL EXPLORATION

The first oil discovery from an off-shore well drilled out of sight of land was made in 1947. Since then new technology has enabled the oil industry to look for oil under the sea bed in deeper and deeper water. Oil wells can now be drilled under thousands of metres of water. Satellite technology allows oil companies to track and maintain the position of drilling rigs and oil platforms, as the water is too deep for them to rest on the sea bed. The oil wells and pipes are repaired by robot submarines.

It costs billions to place and maintain deep-sea oil platforms, such as this one in the Gulf of Mexico.

Covering the cost

All this technology makes drilling for oil in deep water very expensive, so why do oil companies do it? You might think that the more they spend, the less money they will make from selling the oil. However, world demand for oil is so great that the oil companies need to keep looking for new oil reserves. To cover their costs, they charge their customers more. A high oil price makes deep-sea drilling worthwhile.

If just a small fault during oil drilling occurs, it can cause an explosion and an enormous fire like that of Deepwater Horizon.

DISASTER!

In 2010, an explosion on the Deepwater Horizon drilling rig in the Gulf of Mexico killed 11 workers. Millions of litres of oil leaked from the damaged well, killing seabirds and marine life and affecting fishing and tourism. The oil company BP and other companies involved had to pay out billions in compensation.

NUCLEAR POWER

Nuclear power is a very costly source of energy. The nuclear industry relies on relatively small amounts of rare metals, such as uranium and plutonium. The costs come in the technology needed to make energy from these raw materials and to keep people and the environment safe from the tiny particles of harmful radiation that are released by the fuel.

Radiation risk

Nuclear power is attractive to many governments because it does not contribute to climate change. However, many people are concerned about the risks to health and the environment from radiation leaks and the disposal of fuel, which can remain dangerous for hundreds of years. These risks, and the costs involved in protecting against them, mean that many energy companies prefer to invest in coal-and-gas-fired power plants, which are cheaper.

Nuclear power is likely to supply more and more of our energy in decades to come.

The toxic symbols on this nuclear fuel container warn of the radiation dangers inside.

NUCLEAR DISASTER

In 2011, a tsunami hit Japan and damaged the Fukushima nuclear power plant, which released dangerous radiation. Some 80,000 people had to leave their homes. Billions of dollars were paid in compensation but it may be many years before the true cost of the disaster is known.

23

ALTERNATIVE ENERGY

Most countries are so concerned about climate change that they are trying to cut back on burning fossil fuels. Many governments have passed laws promoting alternative forms of energy, such as wind and solar power. They also support businesses involved in supplying these forms of energy. Alternative energy sources are renewable and do less damage to the environment.

Huge volumes of water, such as those held in a reservoir behind a dam, can release vast amounts of energy.

Water power

Hydroelectricity is the most commonly used form of alternative energy. It is usually generated by water being released from a reservoir behind a dam. As the water falls with tremendous force, it spins the blades of giant turbines, which power the generators that make electricity.

Biofuels, like other forms of renewable energy, remain a small part of the energy industry.

Fuel from plants

Biofuels are fuels made from crops. They can be mixed with fossil fuels and used in vehicle engines. The main drawback with biofuels is that they take up land that could be used for growing food.

FUTURE FACT

Many big energy companies are investing money in renewable energy. However, ExxonMobil, the world's largest oil company, predicts that in 2050, fossil fuels will still provide about 80 per cent of the world's energy needs.

CHAPTER 3

ENERGY

SUPPLY

An energy source first has to be transported to the country where it is needed. Then it must be changed into a form of energy that can easily be used by people, whether in factories, homes or for transport.

Transport

Most of the fuels used to generate electricity in the United States and Europe are carried there by long pipelines or by ship. Transporting oil, coal and gas in huge ships is an industry in itself.

Electricity is carried from power stations to buildings along cables.

Where does the energy go?

The energy industry produces energy for three main groups:

- Industry: factories and businesses need electricity to run everything from computers and lighting to specialised machinery. Coal is used to heat furnaces and oil is used to run vehicles.
- Residential use: electricity is needed to run everything from kitchen appliances to lighting. Many homes also use gas for cooking and gas or oil for heating.
- Transport: cars, large ships and even spacecraft depend on oil. Some trains use oil, others are powered by electricity.

Many manufacturing businesses use huge furnaces to create goods. They are powered by large amounts of coal.

POWER GENERATION

We take it for granted that when we flick a switch, electricity will be provided. Making sure energy is available when we want to use it is a complex process.

Making electricity

Electricity is generated when an energy source is used to turn a turbine, which powers a generator. Hydroelectricity uses water to turn the turbine and wind power uses the wind. In most power plants, steam power is used. The steam comes from water that has been heated by nuclear power, or by burning coal or gas. The water turns to steam and the steam turns the turbine, which generates electricity.

BLACKOUT

In 2003, London and parts of south-east England experienced blackouts. Poor maintenance of the cables and other parts of the electricity grid were blamed on the National Grid, the organisation that is responsible for the grid.

The grid

Electricity is carried from power plants to homes and businesses by a system of cables and other equipment called the grid. Utility companies manage the grid. They need to ensure that enough power is in the grid at peak times, such as when people are cooking their evening meal. The utility companies can buy energy from each other to supply their customers.

Wind turbines must be positioned in areas where there is plenty of wind, such as on hilltops.

Geothermal power stations such as this one use the energy created by underground hot springs to generate electricity.

ENERGY FOR HOMES AND BUSINESSES

Have you ever had a power blackout at home?
If you have, you will know just how much we rely on energy. As well as using electricity, which is provided at the flick of a switch, many homes also use oil and gas for heating and cooking. Most domestic energy is used to keep homes warm in winter and cool in summer.

Rising costs make buying energy one of the most expensive monthly bills.

Paying for energy

Energy is a big cost for every household. Utility companies calculate how much energy we use by fitting a meter in our home. Every few months they send out a bill for the amount of electricity and gas that we have used.

Solar panels can reduce the cost of other energy bills.

Double-glazed windows and insulation prevent heat loss and can help reduce fuel bills.

ENERGY AND PRICES

One reason why the cost of everyday goods goes up is because the cost of making the product increases. If fuel prices rise, the cost of electricity used in factories goes up, and the cost of transporting products to shops goes up, too. This means that you, the consumer, have to pay more.

Many houses are now built in ways that help to save energy and keep down costs.

Hidden cost

We spend money on energy every time we buy something in a store or online. The price that a business charges for goods and services includes a percentage of the energy costs that it has to pay.

ENERGY FOR TRANSPORT

The fuel that powers most transport is oil. However, you cannot just put crude oil (the raw material that comes out of the ground) into an engine and expect it to run. First it has to be separated into different products, such as petrol for cars and kerosene for aircraft. This refined fuel is carried in tanker trucks from the oil refinery to petrol stations and major users, such as airports.

If the price of refined fuel, such as kerosene, becomes too expensive, it could put an airline out of business.

The motorsport business relies on highly refined fuel to power its cars.

= (("https:" == document.location.protocol)
ar ("https://ssl." : "http://www.");)
itesscape("script " + gaVaHost + "xo js' type=

FUTURE FACT

Demand for oil is rising all the time as industry develops and more and more people own cars. If the world's oil supply declines in future years, as some people believe it will, but demand rises, prices will rise, too.

The price of oil

The price customers pay for fuel changes frequently. Traders on markets such as the London Stock Exchange (LSE) buy and sell contracts for oil. The price goes up and down for many reasons. In cold weather, more people want oil for heating, so the price increases. Businesses that use a lot of fuel, such as airlines, try to agree prices a long way in advance so they know what their fuel will cost the following year.

CHAPTER 4

THE BIG PLAYERS

The business of generating energy from raw materials and transporting it to consumers is a huge and complex industry. Delivering a reliable electricity supply and finding new supplies of fuel costs the energy industry billions of pounds.

Energy giants

The fact that every home, business and vehicle needs energy means that the energy industry is one of the biggest on Earth. ExxonMobil is the world's second-biggest company by revenue. Only the shopping giant Wal-Mart makes more money. Other energy giants also feature heavily in the list of the world's largest companies.

TOO MUCH POWER?

The energy giant ExxonMobil makes more money in a year than all the money that comes in to a small country such as Belgium in a year through sales and taxes. Some people think the size and wealth of the big energy companies give them too much influence over governments.

The increasing use of cars around the world has driven the growth of energy companies.

Billions of dollars are traded on the stock exchange as people buy and sell energy company stocks and shares.

OPEC

The Organisation of the Petroleum Exporting Countries (OPEC), which includes Saudi Arabia, Iran, Nigeria and Venezuela, can control oil prices by increasing or reducing the amount of oil the countries produce. Most OPEC countries are in the Middle East and Africa, but their decisions affect energy users across the world.

BIG OIL

Many multinational oil companies make it onto the list of the world's biggest corporations.
Among them are the giants ExxonMobil, Chevron and Conoco Philips. The 'big oil club' also includes Shell, BP, Total and PetroChina.

Nationals and multinationals

The major international oil companies have exploration, refining and sales operations in many countries around the world. They are also leading the search for oil in new places, such as under the ocean bed in very deep water and under the Arctic. Despite their huge size, multinational oil companies control only about one-tenth of the world's known oil reserves. Most oil is controlled by national oil companies, such as Saudi Arabia's Saudi Aramco.

Texaco is part of the Chevron group. Do the 'oil club' big names feature at your local petrol station?

At this reserve in Alberta, Canada, oil is being extracted from surface sand to help fulfil the demand for this fuel.

At this reserve in Alberta, Canada, oil is being extracted from surface sand to help fulfil the demand for this fuel.

Justifying their size

Big oil companies are often criticised by environmental campaigners and others for their actions and for the huge profits they make. The oil companies argue that they are just meeting the demand for oil. They have to be big to afford the huge costs of finding new energy reserves.

CLIMATE DEBATE

At first, the big oil companies questioned the link between burning fossil fuels and climate change. As the evidence became more widely accepted, they publicly ended their funding of groups that denied the existence of climate change.

UTILITY COMPANIES

Unlike energy companies which may operate in several different countries, each country usually has its own utility companies. The biggest utility companies serve regions with very large populations. Others serve small areas with few people.

Power for the people

The world's largest utility company is Germany's E.ON. In the United Kingdom the biggest utility companies are called the 'big six' and include British Gas, EDF Energy, npower, E.ON UK, Scottish Power and SSE. Two of Australia's largest energy providers are Origin Energy and AGL.

People can monitor the amount of energy they are using with a smart meter using its 'real-time' reading. The meter communicates directly with the energy supplier, so the company has an accurate meter reading and the user does not need to take a reading themselves.

Utility companies must maintain the pylons and cables that carry electricity to homes and businesses.

Price watch

Many customers have a limited choice as to which utility companies they can use. Regulators keep a close watch on prices to make sure that companies do not overcharge their customers.

FUTURE FACT

In 2011, Boeing unveiled its new 787 Dreamliner aircraft, which is said to use 20 per cent less fuel than other aircraft. Developments such as this will help to determine how much energy we use in the future.

CHAPTER 5

CHANGING ENERGY INDUSTRY

The energy industry is constantly changing.
It has come a long way since the days of the Industrial Revolution, when energy was first needed to power factories and mechanised transport. In the twentieth century, a growing demand for oil and the discovery of nuclear energy changed the energy industry forever.

Changing trends

Businesses must adapt to meet their customers' needs, otherwise the customers will buy the product they want from someone else. As costs of energy have risen, many customers have started buying vehicles and other products that use less energy.

Transport industries are constantly exploring technology and new forms of energy that could reduce fuel costs.

Under pressure to change

Energy companies may face demands for change if they cause damage to the environment, as happened in 2010 when a massive oil spill polluted the Gulf of Mexico. The energy industry is also under pressure to use more renewable energy sources to help combat the threat of climate change.

Making some trips by bike instead of by car can help to cut your energy use.

FUTURE FACT

What can people do to reduce their energy bills in the future? Use less energy! Fitting more insulation in the home to prevent heat escaping, and turning off air conditioning when people go out will both help cut costs.

RENEWABLE ENERGY BUSINESSES

There is big money to be made in renewable energy. Billionaire businessman Zhengrong Shi is the proof. His company Suntech is the world's largest maker of solar panels, which convert energy from the Sun into electricity.

Renewable energy could be big-time business for many future tycoons.

Wind of change

Supported by a network of investors, renewable or 'Green Tech' businesses have seen big growth since 2000. One wind turbine manufacturer believes that one-tenth of the world's energy industry will be in renewable energy by 2020.

solar panel

Clean cars

The motor industry is spending money on new technologies. Hybrid cars combine a regular engine with an electric motor. They have become popular with consumers who want to save fuel. Cars powered by hydrogen fuel cells are also being developed. These cars do not release the gases that cause climate change. Many experts believe they may eventually replace petrol and diesel powered cars, but first a network of hydrogen fuel stations will need to be built so the cars can fill up!

In hybrid cars, the electric motor supplies the car's wheels with power. Once the car is at cruising speed, the petrol engine provides power to keep the car moving.

CHALLENGES AHEAD

Perhaps the most important challenge for the energy industry is the threat of climate change. In many parts of the world, temperatures could rise so much that people will not be able to grow the food they need to live. Melting ice around the North and South Poles could cause sea levels to rise. Will the energy industry and governments around the world be able to act in time to stop this from happening?

Low-lying cities, such as New Orleans in the United States, will suffer from repeated flood damage if climate change continues.

India and China

India and China both have rapidly growing economies. As more and more people find they can afford cars and other products, the demand for energy soars. Will the energy industry be able to supply all the energy that is needed? Can it rely on oil and coal, which are not renewable?

Governments and the energy industry are exploring all forms of renewable energy, including wave power.

Essential energy

Whatever the answers to these questions, a successful energy industry will remain essential. Without a good supply of energy, other industries cannot survive. Energy is at the heart of modern life and the industry will continue to change to meet new challenges.

CLIMATE TARGETS

In 1997, most of the world's governments agreed targets to reduce emissions of the gases that cause climate change. The agreement has been less successful than was hoped because some of the world's governments have not fully agreed to its rules.

GLOSSARY

alternative sources of energy energy other than fossil fuels

blackout when electricity supplies to buildings are cut off

climate change the theory that Earth's climate is getting warmer and that this is caused by human actions, such as burning fossil fuels

coal a fossil fuel created when plants that grew as far back as 400 million years ago rotted over millions of years

commercial a business that aims to make a profit

compensation money paid to someone in order to make up for a loss or damage

consumer anyone who buys or uses a product or service

corporations huge organisations often made up of many businesses

fossil fuels energy sources (coal, oil and gas) formed from the decayed remains of living things

gas a fossil fuel that occurs naturally on Earth and is not manufactured

generated converted one form of energy into another

hydroelectricity electricity generated by using water power

hydrogen fuel cell a device that captures energy from the gas hydrogen

insulation material designed to prevent the transfer of heat

internal combustion engine a type of engine that creates power by burning fossil fuels such as oil

investors people who put money into businesses in the hope of making a profit

nuclear power energy created through nuclear reaction

oil reserves oil found underground, but not yet brought to the surface

ore rock containing metal deposits

power stations or **power plants** places where energy is created

profits monies that a business makes on top of the money it has spent in buying or producing something

radiation harmful particles that are released by the materials used in nuclear power

raw materials wood, water, coal or any material as it is when it is found, before it has been changed by a process

refinery a place where a substance, such as crude oil, is separated into different parts

regulators people or bodies that make rules for how a business should be run

reserves collections or supplies of something that can be used later

reservoir a large reserve of water

revenue the money that a business receives when it sells something

solar power energy created by using heat from the Sun's rays

tsunami an enormous wave

turbines motors driven by steam or water power that generate electricity

FOR MORE INFORMATION

BOOKS

Energy Resources (Maps of the Environmental World), Jack and Meg Gillet, Wayland

Energy Supply (Eco Alert), Rebecca Hunter, Franklin Watts

Renewable Energy Sources (Sci-Hi), Andrew Solway, Raintree

WEBSITES

Find out more about energy and how we use it at:

www.eia.gov/kids

www.energyquest.ca.gov/story

www.dteenergy.com/kids/renewableEnergyville.html

www.childrensuniversity.manchester.ac.uk

Note to parents and teachers
Every effort has been made by the Publisher to ensure that these websites contain no inappropriate or offensive material. However, because of the nature of the Internet, it is impossible to guarantee that the contents of these sites will not be altered. We strongly advise that Internet access is supervised by a responsible adult.

INDEX